Zoom in on
EQUALITY

Heather Moore Niver

E **Enslow Publishing**
101 W. 23rd Street
Suite 240
New York, NY 10011
USA

enslow.com

WORDS TO KNOW

bisexual Describes a person who can fall in love with someone of either sex.

culture A way of life for a group of people.

discrimination Treating people differently because of their age, sex, race, or looks.

diverse Including people from different backgrounds.

gay Describes a person who falls in love with someone of the same sex.

inequality Not being equal.

lesbian A woman who falls in love with another woman.

minority A person from a small group that is different from the larger group. Differences may include race, sex, or religion.

Nazis Members of a group that controlled Germany between 1933 and 1945.

protest To argue against, sometimes in the form of a public activity, like a march.

survey A series of questions that are asked to a large group of people.

white supremacist Someone who believes that white people are better than others.

CONTENTS

We may all look different, but everyone should be treated equally.

The Lesson of the Sneetches

The Sneetches have a problem. In the Dr. Seuss story, some Sneetches have stars on their bellies. Some do not. Which Sneetches are better? Star-Belly Sneetches or Plain-Belly Sneetches? Their arguments end in some silly adventures! Finally, they figure it out. Stars or no stars? Dr. Seuss teaches us that doesn't matter! All Sneetches are really equal.

What Is Equality?

When two things are equal, they are the same in number or quality. When it comes to people, equality means that everyone should have the same opportunities in life. The United States Declaration of Independence is clear. It states that "all men are created equal." It seems pretty simple. People are people. But people have struggled with the idea of equality throughout time. Even today, people argue about it!

Different but Equal

So why does equality matter? It's a tough question. Two things do not need to be exactly the same to be equal. One of the amazing things about human beings is that everyone is

Wheelchair ramps allow people with disabilities to have the same access to places as everyone else.

different! Diversity is what makes our world so interesting! Would you want every flower to look exactly the same? Should every pizza have the same toppings? No, that would be boring!

If we had a world of equality, everyone would have the same chance to succeed. It would mean that every building was built so that wheelchairs could get in. No one would be left out.

Not Okay!
Zero tolerance means refusing to accept certain behavior that is usually negative.

It should not matter if someone is tall or short, has red hair or brown, or whom they love. These differences are what make the world wonderful. And all of the people in it deserve to be treated with respect and equality.

Life Without Equality

There are all different kinds of people. Differences are what make the world interesting. But not everyone sees the beauty in differences. There are all kinds of discrimination. This means that some people are treated differently because of who they are.

Since the days of slavery in the United States, black people have experienced discrimination. Until the civil rights

movement, black people often had separate public restrooms, water fountains, and movie theaters. Until 1965, most black people were unable to vote. It is now illegal to discriminate based on the color of someone's skin, but racial inequality still exists.

Discrimination is not just about race. Sometimes older people are discriminated against just because of their age. They may not be able to do the same things that younger people can. People with disabilities are sometimes not treated as equal. This may be because they can't talk, move, or act like other people.

Fighting for Rights
The civil rights movement was a period in the 1950s and 1960s when people protested the unequal treatment of black people in America.

Women have experienced inequality for a long time. They may not be as big and strong as men. For a long time they were not considered as smart as men. Pregnant women often do not get treated the same as others in the workplace. Other people are discriminated against because they love or marry people of the same sex.

The Holocaust

One historical example of discrimination stands out. It is called the Holocaust. In Germany, millions of people were killed just because they were different. Many of these people were Jewish. Other victims were the mentally and physically disabled, along with anyone who spoke out for them or defended them. The Nazis in Germany did not

During the Holocaust, Jewish people had to wear stars at all times so the Nazis could easily identify them.

like these people. They wanted to rid the world of anyone that was different.

Inequality Today

Sadly, discrimination is still a problem today. In August 2017, white supremacists were marching in Charlottesville, Virginia. Another group objected to their views. They marched in protest. The two groups clashed and fought. One woman died when a car drove into the group of protestors.

White supremacists march in Charlottesville, Virginia, in 2017.

14

Equality Around the World

Often, women are not treated equally. Yet they make up 51 percent of the population! All over the world, women do not have the same opportunities as men. Some girls do not get the same education as boys. Around the globe, millions of girls do not get an education at all. Others are not allowed to play the same sports as boys.

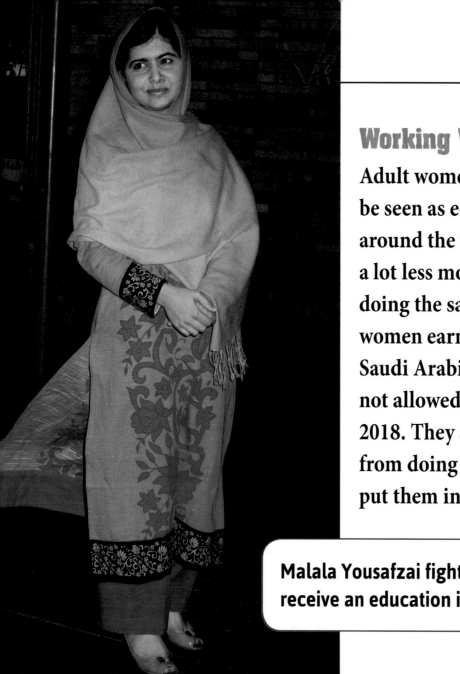

Working Women

Adult women still struggle to be seen as equals, too. Women around the world are paid a lot less money than men doing the same jobs. Minority women earn even less. In Saudi Arabia, women were not allowed to drive cars until 2018. They are also prevented from doing jobs that might put them in contact with men.

Malala Yousafzai fights for girls' rights to receive an education in Pakistan.

More Minorities

Women are not the only minorities who have to fight to gain equality. In school, two-thirds of lesbian, gay, and bisexual students are bullied. Disabled people and some ethnic minorities are a lot less likely to hold important public offices. In the United Kingdom's government, ethnic minorities hold only 27 out of 650 positions.

March for Equality

On January 21, 2017, millions of people from around the world marched in support of women's rights.

The good news is that most people believe equality is very important. For example, people in Great Britain took a survey. It showed that 90 percent of the people disagreed with discriminating against people based on their sexuality.

Everyday Equality

We can work for equality in our daily lives. You don't have to be a powerful person to help others. You can treat them equally. Kids can help! Sometimes it might mean asking an adult for help. Don't be afraid to ask for a hand. Helping one another is an important thing to do!

Understanding

Sometimes people are bullied because they are different. Bullying is never okay. It is important to let an adult know if you see this behavior. Bullies sometimes act unkindly for a reason. They do not understand. People who look or act different may seem threatening. A person may

Bullying can happen when someone is seen as different. Understanding differences is an important part of achieving equality.

not understand another person's culture. He may react by bullying.

Getting to know someone can help. You might be able to help two people get to know each other. This may help them understand each other. Learning about new cultures, beliefs, and other differences helps us respect each other.

Learn the Language!

Is there a student in your class who speaks a different language? Maybe one child speaks better Spanish than English. This is called being bilingual. Try learning a few basic words and simple sentences in Spanish. Or choose another language you don't know. It's not always easy! Try talking to that classmate in his language. Maybe he will help

Once people get beyond their differences, they may find they have a lot in common.

you learn more words. Think about how he feels. Do you think it's hard to learn when everyone else speaks English?

It is important that we try our best to treat everyone equally. The next time you meet someone who looks, acts, or speaks differently, be kind. Don't be afraid to ask questions. You might just make a new friend!

ACTIVITY: NOT SO FAST!

Read the story *The Tortoise and the Hare*. At first, it seems like the hare will win. It's a fast animal! The tortoise is slow. Think about first impressions. Sometimes we label people because of how they look or act. This is called stereotyping. A tortoise could never win a race, right? Not so fast! The tortoise wins the race. What did the other animals expect? How did the tortoise prove them wrong?

How do you think about new people? How do you think about people who are different from you? What could you do in your classroom to make sure everyone is treated equally?

LEARN MORE

Books

Hooks, Gwendolyn, and Kelly Kennedy. *If You Were a Kid During the Civil Rights Movement.* New York, NY: Children's Press/Franklin Watts, 2017.

Martin, Mayah, and Jocelyn Martin. *We Are All the Same: The Bully, the Bullied, and the Brave.* Long Beach, CA: Schoolyard Book Company, 2014.

Seuss, Dr. *The Sneetches and Other Stories.* London, UK: HarperCollins Publishers Children's Books, 2017.

Websites

Stories of Equality

freestoriesforkids.com/tales-for-kids/values-and-virtues/stories-about-equality

Check out this website to read stories about equality.

What Is Diversity?

www.cyh.com/healthtopics/healthtopicdetailskids.aspx?p=335&np=286&id=2345

Learn more about diversity with examples and stories.

INDEX

Published in 2019 by Enslow Publishing, LLC.
101 W. 23rd Street, Suite 240, New York, NY 10011

Copyright © 2019 by Enslow Publishing, LLC.
All rights reserved.

No part of this book may be reproduced by any means without the written permission of the publisher.

Library of Congress Cataloging-in-Publication Data
Names: Niver, Heather Moore, author.
Title: Zoom in on equality / Heather Moore Niver.
Description: New York, NY : Enslow Publishing, 2019. | Series: Zoom in on civic virtues |
  Includes bibliographical references and index. | Audience: Grades K–4.
Identifiers: LCCN 2017045224| ISBN 9780766097636 (library bound) | ISBN
  9780766097643 (pbk.) | ISBN 9780766097650 (6 pack)
Subjects: LCSH: Equality—Juvenile literature. | Citizenship—Juvenile literature.
Classification: LCC HM821 N58 2018 | DDC 305—dc23
LC record available at https://lccn.loc.gov/2017045224

Printed in the United States of America

To Our Readers: We have done our best to make sure all website addresses in this book were active and appropriate when we went to press. However, the author and the publisher have no control over and assume no liability for the material available on those websites or on any websites they may link to. Any comments or suggestions can be sent by e-mail to customerservice@enslow.com.

Photos Credits: Cover, p. 1 Rawpixel.com/Shutterstock.com; p. 4 GagliardiImages/Shutterstock.com; p. 7 Sajee Rod/Shutterstock.com; pp. 10, 13 Bettmann/Getty Images; p. 14 Chet Strange/Getty Images; p. 16 JStone/Shutterstock.com; p. 19 oneinchpunch/Shutterstock.com; p. 21 © iStockphoto.com/monkeybusinessimages; p. 23 Ivy Close Images/Alamy Stock Photo; illustrated children pp. 2, 3, 22, back cover ProStockStudio/Shutterstock.com, pp. 5, 9, 15, 18 MarinaMay/Shutterstock.com.